The ABCs of Brooklyn

An Alphabet Guidebook for All Ages

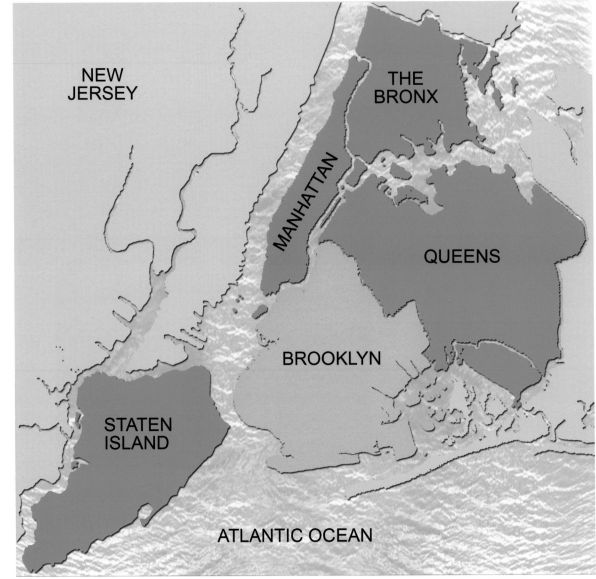

About 375 years ago, Dutch merchants bought land from the Lenape Indians on the western tip of Long Island. They created five towns, one of which they named Breuckelen after a town in Holland. Over time, the name evolved into Brooklyn. In 1664 the British took over the Dutch holdings and created the province of New York. British rule ended with the American victory in the Revolutionary War. Brooklyn remained an independent city until it was consolidated with New York City in 1898. Brooklyn (Kings County) is now the most populous (2.5 million) of the five boroughs of New York City.

A message to adult readers

Brooklyn (Kings County, NY) is physically and demographically large (as populous as Boston, San Francisco, St. Louis and Atlanta combined). Its richness is in the diversity of its people, their neighborhoods, and its colorful history and geography. The folklore and mythology now associated with the word Brooklyn makes it one of the best known place names in the United States.

In *The ABCs of Brooklyn* we tour and celebrate some of the places that are the highlights and icons of this great borough. Given the limitations of a small book for children which illustrates the 26 letters and 11 numbers, we are well aware of what we had to leave out and apologize for those omissions.

A hallmark of this book is its use of language. We have used words and images not commonly associated with alphabet books. As educators and parents, the authors know that children can learn the word "decorative" as readily as "dog" with appropriate guidance from an adult.

Our choice of images and language, including the "footnotes" in light blue type, was guided by our desire to interest the adult as well as the child and to foster a dialogue between them.

Dedicated to our children and grandchildren:

Tamara, Sarah, Daniel,
Dylan, Emily & Tyler
Noah, Liza, Charlie, Luca & Willa

and to all children.

The ABCs of Brooklyn

An Alphabet Guidebook for All Ages

By G. Augustine Lynas
and Peter Vadnai

LYNAS PRESS
NEW YORK CITY

FIRST EDITION

Library of Congress Control Number on request.
Library of Congress-in-Publication data is available upon request.

Printed and bound in Canada by Friesens.

ISBN No. 978-0-9772877-3-4

The ABCs of Brooklyn, An Alphabet Guidebook for All Ages

This book is also available on line at
LynasPress.com or ABCsofBrooklyn.com

Visit us on facebook at The ABCs of Brooklyn

Photo information:

All photographs by Peter Vadnai except where noted.
On front cover, Peter's granddaughter Charlie on the promenade in Brooklyn Heights
On page 1, Empire-Fulton Ferry State Park on the East River between the Manhattan and Brooklyn Bridges
On page 2, A map of NYC boroughs and surrounding area
On title page, A scene at the Brooklyn Children's Museum
On this page, South 6th Street in Brooklyn near the Williamsburg Bridge
Opposite, A random collection of letters all photographed in Brooklyn

Photo on page 16 by Mary Beth Brunner, used with permission.

Aa is for alphabet and the art of advertising with signs in Brooklyn.

Bb is for the big beautiful Brooklyn Bridge and the boat below.

The Brooklyn Bridge is the ultimate icon for Brooklyn and is recognized throughout the world. Its walkways afford wonderful views of New York and the surrounding waterways. Designed by German immigrant John Augustus Roebling in a neo-gothic style, this innovative structure is one of the oldest suspension bridges in the U.S. It took thirteen years to build and was opened in 1883.

Cc is for cute children concentrating at Coney Island beach.

When the Brooklyn Rapid Transit Company electrified the steam railroads and connected Brooklyn to Manhattan at the beginning of the 20th century, Coney Island became accessible to day-trippers who wanted to escape the summer heat. With nearly three miles of sandy beach on the Atlantic Ocean, numerous amusement parks, a boardwalk, a minor league baseball stadium and a first-class aquarium, Coney Island is a fun-filled destination in any season.

Dd is for a dramatic, decorative doorway design.

Every year, more than a million visitors pass through these Brooklyn Public Library doors which opened to the public in 1941. It is one of New York's most impressive Art Deco buildings, occupies more than 350,000 square feet and contains more than a million books, magazines, and multimedia materials. The children's section is a popular destination for Brooklyn's preschoolers.

Ee is for elevated train tracks that use electrical energy.

Starting in 1899, various companies operated rapid transit lines in New York City, at first, only as elevated railways with steam locomotives. These elevated lines made distant neighborhoods like this Brighton Beach area more easily accessible. Granville T. Woods, an African-American inventor, created the third-rail system for providing electric power to railway cars. His invention was successfully demonstrated at Coney Island. Riding the elevated trains is also fun.

Ff is for a fancy facade with fine features.

The Brooklyn Academy of Music (BAM) currently contains movie theaters, an opera house, live theaters and a café. BAM is the heart and soul of the exciting and expanding BAM Cultural District in Ft. Greene. The Brooklyn Academy of Music was originally the home of the Philharmonic Society of Brooklyn. The original building in Brooklyn Heights was destroyed by fire in 1903 and the present home was built in 1908.

Gg is for a gorgeous glass greenhouse in the garden.

The Victorian style greenhouse known as The Palm House is an event venue at the Brooklyn Botanic Garden. In front of the greenhouse is the Lilly Pool Terrace where, in warm weather, visitors can see nearly 100 varieties of hardy and tropical water-lilies, elegant sacred lotuses, and other aquatic plants.

Hh is for huge high-rise offices and homes hiding the horizon.

The invention of the elevator and the use of reinforced concrete made taller buildings easier to construct and has consolidated the infrastructure and the lives of Brooklyn's people. Its downtown neighborhood has become a vital and lively urban center whose skyline rivals that of many American cities. This is truly a mixed neighborhood of offices, residences, government buildings and stores rife for exploration.

Ii is for impressive iron and inverted images in the water.

These cranes dating from the late 1930s have been preserved as icons of a bygone era. Working barges and tugboats can still be seen from Erie Basin Park at the foot of Dwight Street in Red Hook. There are artifacts and interpretive materials about shipbuilding and repair throughout the park. It's a wonderful place to stroll or picnic while watching the busy New York harbor.

Jj is for just one horse and rider on a jaunt by Jamaica Bay.

Jamaica Bay is a wildlife refuge composed of the open water of Jamaica Bay and the intertidal salt marsh. The refuge is entirely within the boundaries of New York City. The salt marshes offer prime habitat for migratory birds and other wildlife. Most of the waters and marshes have been protected since 1972 as part of the Gateway National Recreation Area. The family-owned Jamaica Bay Riding Academy offers 500 acres of horseback riding trails and parent led pony rides for children under age eight.

Photo by Mary Beth Brunner

Kk is for knowing Kings County (Brooklyn) as seen from space.

Kings County was named by the British after their King Charles II. This photograph was shot from space by NASA. It shows four of the five boroughs of New York City including: the southern tip of Manhattan Island, about half of Queens, much of Staten Island, none of the Bronx, and a small part of New Jersey. It also shows Governor's Island, Liberty Island and Ellis Island. The red line describes Brooklyn. Prospect Park, Floyd Bennett Field and several bridges are also visible.

KINGS COUNTY

L l is for learning lessons under lovely limbs.

The Cherry Esplanade is a broad green field bordered by two allées of the dazzling Prunus 'Kanzan'. Cherry Walk was planted in 1921 and soon became known as one of the best cherry blossom viewing sites outside of Japan. These double-flowering cherries typically bloom at the end of April and are a highlight of the Garden's annual cherry blossom festival. The Esplanade is the only part of the Brooklyn Botanic Garden where visitors can sit on the grass and even enjoy a picnic.

Mm is for monument in memory of many men and women.

The Soldiers' and Sailors' Memorial Arch at Grand Army Plaza is at the entrance of Prospect Park and the Brooklyn Public Library. It stands at the center of a traffic circle where eight busy streets converge. The arch was designed by John H. Duncan in a style similar to the *Arc de Triomphe* in Paris and honors the casualties of the Amirican Civil War.

Nn is for nice evening light shining on a New York neighborhood.

This twilight image of Fort Greene is one of Brooklyn's many "home towns." (*See pages 46-47.*) Many of the neighborhoods and their Dutch names come from pre-revolutionary times. Although there are no official borders, most Brooklynites believe they know their own neighborhood's boundaries.

Oo is for orange seats, the orange D sign and outside views.

The D train crosses the East River on the Manhattan Bridge giving spectacular views of the skylines of Manhattan and Brooklyn as well as the Brooklyn and Williamsburg Bridges. The D train travels all the way from the Bronx to Coney Island.

Pp is for a petite person with a purple balloon on the promenade.

Above the Brooklyn-Queens Expressway is a promenade that affords one of the best views of lower Manhattan anywhere. Park benches under mature trees, near expensive Brooklyn Heights homes, attract people who can stroll or relax and watch the sun go down behind the Statue of Liberty. Near the foot of the Brooklyn Bridge, the Promenade is close to the old cobble stone streets of historic Brooklyn Heights and its famous restaurants, book store, shops and parks.

Qq is for quaint, quiet places like Green-Wood Cemetery.

The Green-Wood Cemetery was founded in 1838 soon brought about half a million visitors a year to its splendid 478 acres. It became one of Brooklyn's most popular tourist attraction as a place for quiet outings. Green-Wood's popularity inspired the creation of more public parks, including New York City's Central Park and Brooklyn's Prospect Park.

Rr is for restored row houses and repeating railings.

This landmarked street is typical of many in Brooklyn neighborhoods. Originally built to save money, row houses are now highly sought. Many have been lovingly restored. A walk through Brooklyn can be like a walk through an architecture museum where styles such as Federal, Greek Revival, Gothic Revival, Second Empire, and the eclectic, picturesque styles of the late nineteenth and early twentieth centuries can be found.

Ss is for sculptures at a special school on a sunny day.

Pratt Institute, founded by industrialist Charles Pratt in 1887, is one of the leading private art schools in the U.S. Almost 900 staff and faculty and nearly 5,000 students work on its 25-acre campus in Clinton Hill, Brooklyn. The oldest continually functioning elevator in all of Brooklyn was installed in 1910. Pratt also has the oldest continuously operating, privately owned, steam-powered electric generating plant in the U.S. The campus is an inviting, sculpture-filled oasis open to the general public.

Tt is for trucks, traffic and a tall tower that tells time.

The former Williamsburg Savings Bank (here viewed from Flatbush Ave.) is now a condominium residence called One Hanson Place. The 512-foot tower was the tallest building in Brooklyn for seventy years. It is distinguished by its four-sided clock tower and golden dome. Its exterior and the bank interior are both New York City landmarks. With its soaring ceiling, mosaics, marble floors, elaborate iron-work and sculptures, the bank resembles a cathedral and is well worth a visit.

Uu is for under the unique urban overpass.

DUMBO (Down Under the Manhattan Bridge Overpass) is the place to be if you're interested in what's happening in art, music, dining and night life in New York. Visit the new Empire-Fulton Ferry State Park where Washington and Main Streets meet the East River. Here you can enjoy great river views, playgrounds, picnics, planned events or just strolling along the water's edge.

Vv is for views of the Verrazano Bridge from very high vantage points.

This huge bridge spans the narrows between Staten Island and Bay Ridge / Ft. Hamilton, Brooklyn. It bears the name of Giovanni Verrazano who was the first-known European to navigate New York harbor and the Hudson River. Actually called the Verrazano-Narrows Bridge, it was the longest suspension bridge in the world for seventeen years after its completion in 1964. It has been the starting point of the NYC Marathon since 1976.

Ww is for waves and the waterfront where warehouses once were.

For decades, much of this part of the Brooklyn waterfront (known as DUMBO) had been inaccessible for the enjoyment of the general public. This spectacular area between the Manhattan and Brooklyn bridges is now the site of residences and the new Empire-Fulton Ferry State Park.

Xx is for the name of this avenue.

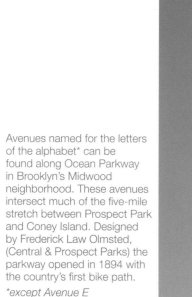

Avenues named for the letters of the alphabet* can be found along Ocean Parkway in Brooklyn's Midwood neighborhood. These avenues intersect much of the five-mile stretch between Prospect Park and Coney Island. Designed by Frederick Law Olmsted, (Central & Prospect Parks) the parkway opened in 1894 with the country's first bike path.

*except Avenue E

Yy is for this young, yellow elephant yelling with joy.

This ride is one of the many colorful attractions at the Coney Island amusement area. Others include: the famous Boardwalk, the Cyclone, the Wonder Wheel, the New York Aquarium, and a minor league baseball stadium. The Native American Lenape people referred to Coney Island Beach as the land without shadows because the beach is in sunlight all day.

Zz

is for zoo, zoology and also for zero zebras in this photo.

The twelve-acre Prospect Park Zoo is on Flatbush Avenue across from the Brooklyn Botanic Garden. As part of the Wildlife Conservation Society, the zoo features three major exhibits: The World of Animals, Animal Lifestyles, and Animals in Our Lives. There are outdoor paths, interactive and interpretive materials for all ages. In addition, the zoo's Discovery Center provides classrooms and labs where children are introduced to the work of environmental and wildlife science.

Here are 10 numerals from signs found all over Brooklyn.
With these 10 numerals, any number in the world can be made.

Beautifully restored in 2000, the three -acre Japanese Hill-and-Pond Garden opened in 1915. It was the first Japanese garden to be created in an American public garden. It is considered to be a masterpiece of Japanese landscape designer Takeo Shiota. Artificially constructed hills, a waterfall, pond, and an island are designed to reveal various natural elements on winding pathways. Visitors will discover wooden bridges, lanterns, a pavilion, a gateway, and a shrine.

purple costume in a popular people's parade

On Labor Day the annual West Indian-American Day Carnival wends its way down Eastern Parkway as huge numbers of masqueraders and celebrants dance along miles of the Parkway. Flanked by dense crowds of onlookers, floats loaded with and surrounded by elaborately costumed celebrants illustrate a theme chosen for that year.

Sheepshead Bay, which separates Brooklyn from Coney Island, was named for the sheepshead, a fish once found in the local waters. It is the home port of a recreational fishing fleet. A Holocaust memorial park, used for commemorative events, is at the Western end of the bay. Russian-style restaurants, nightclubs and new condominiums proliferate. Emmons Avenue, the shoreline street along the bay, has piers with tour boats and a seafood market.

3 bay windows on a spring morning

Brooklyn architecture ranges from a log cabin in Canarsie to glass and steel high-rises in downtown. Many other styles including large mansions, row houses, brownstones, big apartment buildings and clapboard, single family homes like these can be found. Bay windows provide light, seating and side views of the street. Exploring Brooklyn's varied architectural styles is fun and a good way to encourage discussions of our history.

4 blue-gray horse statues on the monument

These bronze sculptures atop the Soldiers' and Sailors' Memorial Arch by Brooklyn-born Frederick MacMonnies, represent a four-horse chariot driven by Columbia (meaning America), who is flanked by Victory blowing trumpets. It can be seen up close in the spring and fall when the parks department opens a stairway to the roof of the arch.

It took five years to build Brooklyn's City Hall. Forty-nine years later Brooklyn became part of New York City and Kings County became the Borough of Brooklyn. In 1895 fire and water destroyed and damaged the upper floors. In the 1980s the building was restored and added to the National Register of Historic Places.

6 warm-gray columns on the Brooklyn Museum

About a half million people a year visit the Brooklyn Museum to see art from all over the world, from ancient cultures to contemporary works. Opened in 1897, the building is one quarter the size of its original plan due to New York City's budget cuts. In 2004, the new pavilion was added to the Eastern Parkway entrance. The museum holds many free events for families.

7 colorful boats at the children's museum

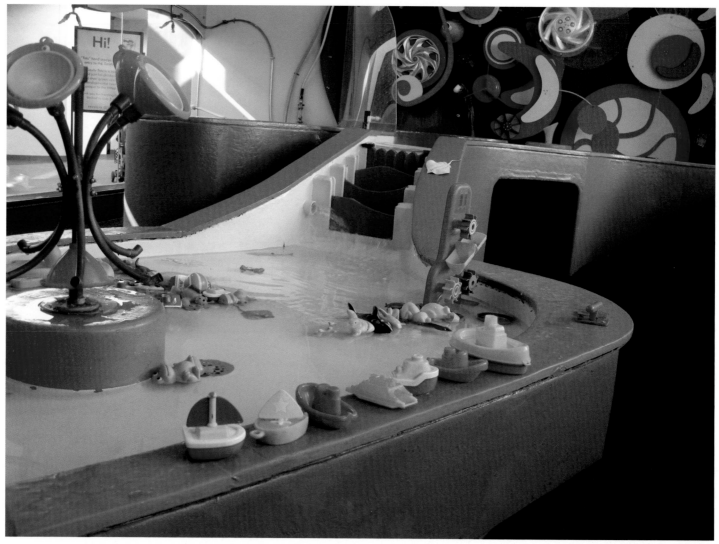

This water play area is in the toddler section of the The Brooklyn Children's Museum. The museum was perhaps the very first in the U.S. devoted entirely to children. Located at 145 Brooklyn Avenue, in a mostly residential neighborhood, the museum expanded to double its original size in 2005. It uses geothermal energy for heat and cooling.

8 stoops and 8 cars on the street as the sun sets

Stoop, from the Dutch word *stoep,* means (small porch or step) has come to represent the steps in front of most row houses. The stoop is where, in warm weather, neighbors hang out to exchange gossip and where kids would play "stoop ball." In the game, a rubber ball is pitched against the stoop to make it bounce as high and far as possible so that fielders couldn't catch it before it hit the ground.

9 total letters and numbers on the bus route sign

The New York Transit Museum is in the historic 1936 IND subway station in downtown Brooklyn (130 Livingston Street). The museum features vintage subway cars, buses and numerous artifacts from the development of the largest transportation network in North America. Many interactive exhibits such as this 1960's refurbished bus cab are appropriate for children of all ages to enjoy.

10 tempting, cherry cheesecakes in Junior's window

Located at the corner of Flatbush and DeKalb Avenues, Junior's Restaurant has been serving it's famous cheesecakes since 1929 when it was known as Enduro's Sandwich Shop. Cheesecake was already a popular dish in ancient Greece before Romans adopted it. In 1912, James Kraft invented a form of pasteurized cream cheese which is now the most commonly used cheese for making cheesecake.

Manhattan

Queens

Brooklyn Neighborhoods

Greenpoint

Williamsburg

East
Williamsburg

DUMBO

Downtown

Northern
Brooklyn

Bushwick

Brooklyn
Heights

Cobble
Hill

Fort
Greene

Clinton
Hill

Boerum
Hill

Carroll
Gardens

Bedford Stuyvesant

Cypress
Hills

Red
Hook

Prospect
Heights

City
Line

Gowanus

Park
Slope

Crown Heights

Brownsville

East New York

Prospect
Park

Prospect
Lefferts
Gardens

Bush

Windsor

Here are some well-known Brooklyn neighborhoods, along with a few major landmarksl. We split ther map into halves to fit the format of the book.

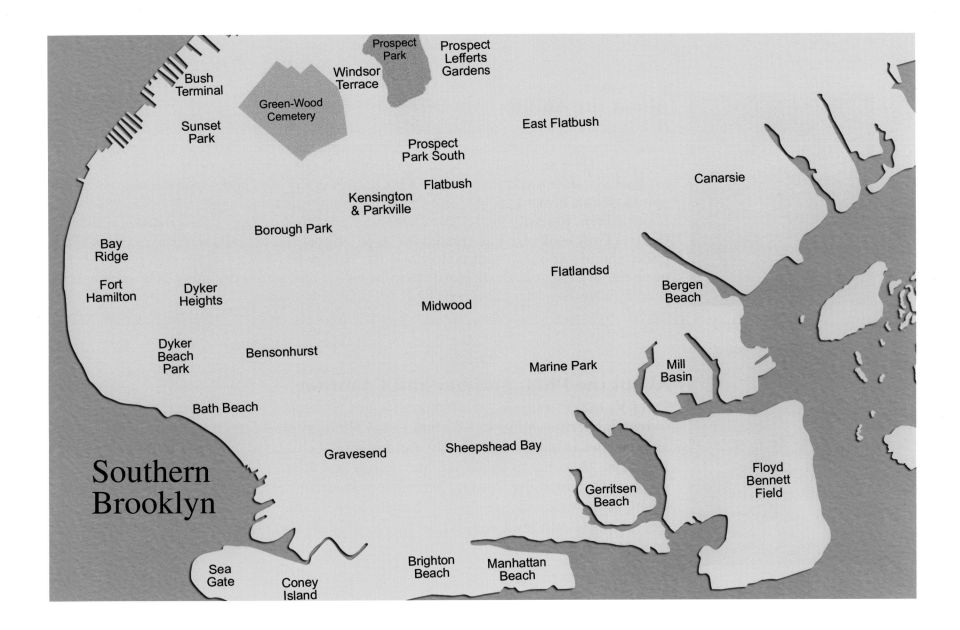

Bush
Terminal

Prospect
Park

Prospect
Lefferts
Gardens

Windsor
Terrace

Green-Wood
Cemetery

Sunset
Park

East Flatbush

Prospect
Park South

Flatbush

Canarsie

Kensington
& Parkville

Borough Park

Bay
Ridge

Flatlandsd

Fort
Hamilton

Dyker
Heights

Bergen
Beach

Midwood

Dyker
Beach
Park

Bensonhurst

Marine Park

Mill
Basin

Bath Beach

Gravesend

Sheepshead Bay

**Southern
Brooklyn**

Floyd
Bennett
Field

Gerritsen
Beach

Sea
Gate

Brighton
Beach

Manhattan
Beach

Coney
Island

About the Author / Art Director / Designer

G. Augustine Lynas is a freelance artist / author who has lived and worked in New York City since 1965. Although he is an experienced graphic designer, his first love is sculpture. He gained worldwide recognition as a sand sculptor with the publication of his book *Sandsong* and the release of his documentary film of the same name. Mr. Lynas paints, draws, designs games, and writes and illustrates books including *The ABCs of Central Park*. Recently he designed *ABC San Antonio* for Stage Books (based on the Central Park book). He has created concrete, bronze and ceramic sculptures in six NYC parks and in various private collections. For twenty years Mr. Lynas was an adjunct professor of Design at Pratt Institute in Brooklyn and tutors privately. His work can be seen at www.SandSong.com and at www.LynasPress.com

About the Photographer and Coauthor

Peter Vadnai is a professional photographer who has specialized in corporate and industrial photography. In addition to his photographic career, he spent several years as a teacher in public schools. He and his grown children and their families live in Brooklyn. He came to Brooklyn later in life and found an endless source of artistic inspiration, fun and surprises. Peter set aside his professional cameras and lighting for his favorite point-and-shoot camera and available light to capture the joys of Brooklyn. He and Mr. Lynas have collaborated on several projects and are close friends.